Anglesey
A Megalithic Journey

Neil McDonald

mutusliber

London

First published in 2010 by Mutus Liber

BM Mutus Liber
London WC1N 3XX

A CIP catalogue record for this book is available from
the British Library.

ISBN-13: 978-0-9555230-6-9

www.mutusliber.com

Contents

Introduction

The main approach route to the mystical Isle of Anglesey is by
the old road, which winds its way along the north coast of
Wales, passing signs bearing town names remembered from
childhood Welsh holidays, such as Llandudno, Prestatyn and
Rhyl. On passing the walled town of Conwy, the road
traverses a huge mountainous boulder and you catch the first
sight of your destination on the horizon. This is Penmon Point,
a place of very early settlement and a place we will soon visit.

On a tour I always point out this breath-taking view of the
peninsula and island across Conwy Bay and am always met
with gasps of awe as the collective morale soars, especially after
a long journey.

Evidence has been found of human inhabitation on the island
as long ago as the Mesolithic period, around 7,000 BC, but
continuous occupation may have begun much earlier.

Anglesey is separated from the main land by a narrow stretch
of sea, known as the Menai Strait or 'Afon Menai' in Welsh. In
the first century AD, when the island had been a stronghold of
the religious and mystical sect of Druidism, it was this wide
and treacherous channel which had been enough to enable the
Druids to fend off the encroaching Roman invaders until a
final and furious standoff. In 60 AD the Roman legions faced
the terrifying sight of the painted warring Druids across the

strait. The Roman historian Tacitus wrote of the ensuing battle scene:

"On the beach stood the adverse array [of Britons], a serried mass of arms and men, with women flitting between the ranks. In the style of Furies, in robes of deathly black and with dishevelled hair, they brandished their torches; while a circle of Druids, lifting their hands to heaven and showering imprecations, struck the troops with such awe at the extraordinary spectacle that, as though their limbs were paralysed, they exposed their bodies to wounds without an attempt at movement. Then, reassured by their general, and inciting each other never to flinch before a band of females and fanatics, they charged behind the standards, cut down all who met them, and enveloped the enemy in his own flames. The next step was to install a garrison among the conquered population, and to demolish the groves consecrated to their savage cults; for they considered it a pious duty to slake the altars with captive blood and to consult their deities by means of human entrails."[1]

The Roman victory which eventually followed was a hollow one, as in order to take on the Druids they had left the South of England relatively undefended, providing Boudica with just the opportunity she had been waiting for. In the absence of the Roman legions she mobilised her armies southwards and sacked London, Winchester and other Roman fortifications, thus drawing the Roman legions south again and so away from Anglesey.

For the next 1,766 years the only way to get to the island was by fighting the hazardously strong currents of the Strait and many ferries were lost making the journey. In 1785 a boat carrying 55 people became stranded on a sandbank with the

---

[1] John Jackson, translator. William Heinemann Press, 1951.

loss of all but one life. Then in 1826 the opening of Thomas Telford's impressive Menai Strait suspension bridge provided an opulent first direct access to the island. In 1850 Robert Stevenson's Britannia Bridge was added and today the island is still connected to North Wales by these two magnificent bridges.

Present-day visitors to Anglesey find a beautiful and varied landscape with rugged coastlines, wonderful sea views and a warm and friendly welcome. My visits have always left me with the feeling that (as on the Isle of Man) something is going on behind the scenes and that the locals know something I don't. In fact I have been told on numerous occasions that the 'old ways' are still practised extensively throughout the island by these people that remain that much closer to the land than us townies.

The Menai Strait Bridge

Today we find an assortment of ancient and sacred sites dotted throughout the island including standing stones, burial sites, wells and ancient settlements. We will start our exploration by visiting the most important Welsh prehistoric site, the chambered tomb of Bryn Celli Ddu.

This site lies within a sacred landscape which could have been used by the ancients for millennia for religious ceremony and ritual practice. The surrounding landscape is littered with various alignments which link places of early gathering, such as rocky outcrops with standing stones, burial chambers and henges and possibly connecting places of distinctive earth energy.

Other theories connect chambered tombs with celestial alignments and places of refuge in times of severe natural disaster. These cromlechs or burial chambers which are sprinkled across the island were not simply Neolithic cemeteries but were places of extreme importance for religious ritual and ceremony. This could have included the removal and relocation of bones in an orderly and symbolic manner and also the rebuilding and destruction of the entrance to symbolise death and rebirth to coincide with the wheel of the seasons of the year.

Anglesey is an island of a manageable 290 square miles, with a width of 23 miles across at the widest axis of south-east to north-west and with a population of around 67,000 people before the influx of tourism in the summer months. For the first two or three thousand years of early settlement, the areas of the island away from the coast were covered with dense oak and hazel forests, a scene very different to the wide open landscapes seen today. The following chapters will take the reader on a circular tour around a selection of some of the most interesting and important ancient and historical sites of the island.

1. Bryn Celli Ddu Chambered Tomb
OS-114-507702

Bryn Celli Ddu Chambered Tomb

You can just about make out Bryn Celli Ddu, or 'Brin Kethlee Thee' as it is pronounced, from the road if you know which way to look, but getting to the site involves a ten minute walk along a well-defined and apparently purpose-built track-way. You follow a stream and cross a small wooden bridge, give it a couple of turns and there it sits waiting in its own fenced-off area surrounded by sheep and cattle.

This magnificent chambered tomb provides a 'wow factor' at first sight and you can't wait to find what is hidden inside this impressive mound. The site lies within a larger ceremonial landscape and is one of the most important sacred places not only in Wales in all of Britain.

Although translation of the name cannot be accurately carried out, it means something like 'the mound in the grove of the deity'. But the site is also deservedly known as the 'Stonehenge of the North', which indicates not only its importance but, like its more well-known counterpart, a period of continuous development and construction. It began life as a man-made structure in the early Neolithic Age as a henge meeting place, with a stone circle built inside it.

When you arrive at what is now the main site, a look over to the northwest will reveal a natural rocky outcrop known as a Gorsedd or 'throne'. This proto-temple, as Julian Cope described it,[2] would, I believe, have been the original sacred meeting place long before the henge was constructed. Although the field holding the Gorsedd is fenced off, it is possible to make out the flat worn surface of the outcrop which would indicate usage over an extremely long period. In the same field as the Gorsedd, a further 200 yards to the south, is a standing stone, which marks the direction of an alignment which carries on through the nearby Llandaniel Fab Standing Stone and on to the village of Llandaniel Fab.

The original bank and henge had a diameter of 57 feet with the standing stones situated within the henge. This is a form of construction which can be seen at sites throughout Britain, including Stonehenge. The stones were removed by the late Neolithic people, who then built a tomb in the centre and it is this which we see today as the main site. The one remaining stone is actually a cast of the original, which now stands in the National Museum of Wales in Cardiff.

The chambered tomb dome, which is now the centerpiece of Bryn Celli Ddu, is a magnificent sight containing a 27 foot passageway leading into a small chamber. The chamber was

---

[2] Julian Cope, *The Modern Antiquarian*, Pg.111, Thorsons, 1998.

first broken into in 1699 by a group who dug through the outer mound in the dead of night and on entering the main open area shone the light from their lantern around the newly uncovered chamber catching sight of the carved standing stone within. It is said that they were so filled with terror that they fled off across the fields without looking back.

It is the secrets of this intriguing chamber that caused me to pay a visit to Bryn Celli Ddu one dark night just after the winter solstice of 2006 and I can confirm that things can get a little spooky, even if it is only as a result of the sound of grass munching from invisible live stock.

The reason for my nocturnal expedition was mainly to experience the 'Venus factor', a planet that has proved so important in my esoteric studies over so many years. If you were to plot Venus's cyclic journey through the heavens on a map, the various positions the planet occupies would form a perfect pentagram, a symbol of immense importance in some of the earliest spiritual teachings. Still today the pentagram holds great meaning to many as having spiritual significance, with the upper most point of the pentagram representing the spiritual life, standing above the remaining lower four points which represent the four elements which make up the physical universe.

The only natural light in the skies of course is the sun, with all other lights being a reflection of this solar body. At the summer solstice, as the sun rises, it shines directly down the passageway at Bryn Celli Ddu and illuminates the main chamber. This indication of the summer solstice would have been an important marker to our ancestors for religious, agricultural and probably social purposes and may have signified the arrival of the time for great celebration.

The second most reflective body in the heavens, after the moon, is Venus and it is at the winter solstice that this planet shows its reflective presence at Bryn Celli Ddu. As it progresses through its cycle, Venus appears as an evening star around half of the time; during the remainder, as a morning star. The builders of this amazing chamber were clearly well aware of this and incorporated it as an integral part of the design. Around the winter solstice as the sun sets, it shines a beam of light through a slot in the back of the site, causing a dagger of light to form on the inner chamber's resident standing stone, which dissipates as the sun sets. Then, at certain times of its cycle, Venus provides a further beam of light on the standing stone just over an hour later until the planet eventually follows the Sun over the horizon. By calculating the relative position of the two beams of light on the pillar it is possible to fix the year's solar calendar. This clock was set over 5,000 years ago and it is still going today; what's more it does not need winding as it runs on solar power.

The pictures below show the sun going down behind Bryn Celli Ddu and the lighted chambers, from my visit at the winter solstice of 2006.[3]

The sun going down behind Bryn Celli Ddu

[3] See also Christopher Knight and Robert Lomas, *Uriel's Machine*, Pg. 328/329, Arrow Books, 2000.

My few hours at Bryn Celli Ddu in the dead of winter were cold and somewhat scary, but I now have some insight into the minds of those early 1699 visitors. And I would not have missed this magical experience for anything.

Sunset as seen from inside the chamber

2. Bodowyr Cromlech
OS-114-462683

Bodowyr Cromlech

Driving around Anglesey and searching out its wonderful collection of ancient sites involves negotiating narrow farm tracks with high banks and hedgerows, reminiscent of Cornwall's Land's End peninsula. The landscape is so similar in places that it is possible to confuse the roads, expecting a left turn after the next bend and then realizing that the remembered road is in fact over 200 miles away.

A good knowledge of the roads, lanes and track-ways of this resplendent landscape would be a great help in locating some of the island's smaller examples of ancient cromlechs, standing stone and megaliths, as they hide silently in fields behind high hedgerow barriers.

Usually the first thing you see that gives away the location of a nearby megalithic site is a government information board next to a small stile; arriving at Bodowyr Cromlech (pronounced 'Bod-owe-er') is no exception. You find yourself squeezing your vehicle as tightly into the side of the narrow lane as you can manage without removing the paintwork and without forcing passengers into patches of nettles ready to cause irritation to unwary travellers. You then climb the stile and there it is, an exquisite little mushroom-like structure and a fine example of a well-preserved chambered tomb. Like many Anglesey monuments, Bodowyr is kept within a fenced-off area which protects it from animals, intent on using its upright stones as scratching posts. Unusually the fence surrounding Bodowyr has no gate so it is impossible to get up close and personal. It could very well be that the site is considered unsafe for visitors to climb inside and to say that the capstone appears a little precarious would be a huge understatement.

Starting an exploration of Anglesey at Bryn Celli Ddu is always a good idea as it provides an idea of what a completed chambered tomb or cromlech would have looked like. Today, due to centuries of farming, Bodowyr has totally lost its covering curbstones and, as with many of its kind, lies bare to the elements. If you carry on walking past the site for a couple of minutes you come across a pile of stones, which are probably there as a result of the farmer combing the field to remove rocks. This always leaves visitors wondering if the stones were once part of the cromlech, or even part of a further site which has now disappeared. When I run tours to Anglesey I always make a point of not mentioning these outlying rocks but invariably they are noticed by the groups, who tend to enjoy speculating on the possibility of an extended site at Bodowyr. This could well be the case, but unfortunately it is probably too late to make any real discoveries after so many years of farming and plowing activity.

Today it is left to the imagination to go back 5,000 years and to build up a picture of the complete cromlech with its covering of curbstones and earth. You do still have a reasonable amount to work from, with the arched capstone which is 8 feet by 6 feet and balanced precariously on three supporting posts of 4 and 5 feet high. A fourth upright is still in place, but this one no longer reaches the capstone and a further megalithic support has fallen and lies just outside.

It has been suggested by Julian Cope[4] that this dolmen's shape once defined the body of the landscape goddess, for the name Bodowyr translates as 'the body or existence of Ur', literally 'Bod O Ur', and the name 'Ur' has long been associated with an earth deity.

The site has never been excavated so no artifacts have ever been reported but it is well worth noting the seams of quartz on the underside of the capstone and one of the posts.

---

[4] Julian Cope, *The Modern Antiquarian*, Pg. 304, Thorsons, 1998.

3. Bryn Gwyn Tre'r Dryw Circle Portal Stones and Bryn Gwyn Castell Henge
OS-114-464671

On entering Anglesey by the Menai Strait Bridge it is possible to traverse the whole of the Island by the coast road before finally leaving by the Britannia Bridge. This is a good way to visit the various sites, as many lie not far inland and take only a small detour from the main orbital road before rejoining to cover the next stretch. The views from the coast road are breathtaking throughout, but from the eastern section you get the added bonus of the Snowdonia mountain range forming a panoramic vista of the distant mainland across the Menai Strait.

It is from this road that I first came across a small easily missed sign pointing out 'Castell Bryn Gwyn' down a narrow farm track. I had missed this site in my earlier research and it was not on my agenda for the day, but always being one for a quest, off I went. The lane was tranquil with the usual high sides and the flies swarmed as it twisted and turned once or twice passing small farms until after 12 minutes or so there it was: an obvious henge on the left. Yes, I thought sitting on the henge bank and looking over the almost complete circle, I like this!

Castell Bryn Gwyn put me in the mind of other such sites across Britain and in particular King Arthur's Round Table henge in Cumbria and I began to wonder if the two nearby standing stones of Bryn Gwyn Tre'r Dryw I had been searching for would be in any way associated with this site. This idea led me back to the coast road to investigate.

Sure enough a few hundred yards down the road there they were, standing proud yet curiously camouflaged in a muddy cattle field near a large thorn hedge. On approaching the stones I had two overriding thoughts, firstly can I reach the stones through what must be the deepest mud in Britain and secondly these two seemingly separate sites must be part of the same sacred design.

On returning home it did not take long before I realized that I was not the first to think this way. As far back as 1723 Henry Rowlands had produced a suggested layout of the original sites,[5] and William Stukeley had also produced a similar reconstruction.[6]

It is always a great pity when wonderful sacred landscapes such as these are so extensively damaged but, as usual, a certain amount of imagination can bring the past back to life. If you can picture a huge flat circular plain with Bryn Gwyn Tre'r Dryw as a large and prominent stone circle at one end, with a processional way leading to the nearby Castell Bryn Gwyn henge and ditch at the other, I think you would not be far off the mark. The whole thing would have been surrounded by a dense forest, with cairns and standing stones at significant points.

Castell Bryn Gwyn (White Hill Castle)
OS-114-464671

The usage of the word 'castle' for Bronze Age sites throughout Britain can be somewhat misleading and Castell Bryn Gwyn did not begin its life as a castle when it was first constructed in the late Neolithic or early Bronze Age. We tend to associate the word 'castle' with military strength – sieges, wars and so on – and it is a pity that we seem to find it difficult to imagine a time

---

[5] Henry Rowlands, *Mona Antiqua Restaurata*, Kessinger Publishing, 2008.
[6] William Stukeley, *Itinerarium Curiosum*, 2nd edition, republished, London: Baker & Leigh, 1776.

when people could have lived together in harmony and have constructed places such as Castell Bryn Gwyn for peaceful meeting. Another misleading feature of this site is the external ditch, suggestive of a moat, in contrast to many such henge monuments throughout Britain, although it is not unique.

Excavations in 1960 revealed post holes indicating a second lease of life, probably in the Iron Age, when the site was inhabited and defensive encampments and fortifications were constructed, as would have been required at the time. It could have been this that led to the castle appellation.

The tranquil track-way to the site is only surpassed by the arriving. The henge at Castell Bryn Gwyn is serene, atmospheric and well formed, or at least this is true of the portion that still remains, as alas a farm house was built across the northern section of the site in 1872, covering the location of one of the entrances. This unfortunate construction is not as bad as you might first think and it does not appear to detract much from the site's rather distinctive atmosphere and energy. The house has always proved an interesting talking point for visitors imagining how it would be to live inside an ancient site.

The opportunity of moving to Avebury, which is the only village in Britain to be actually inside a stone circle, will not present itself to many of us, but something like the farmhouse here might be possible and much more undisturbed, being away from the hordes of visitors who make their way to the better known sites. As for megalithic travelers, this site seems to instinctively lead to a spell of dowsing practice.

Bryn Gwyn Tre'r Dryw
OS-114-462669

The Bryn Gwyn Tre'r Dryw stones

Bryn Gwyn Tre'r Dryw (pronounced 'Brin Gwin Trair Droo'), lying 440 yards west-south-west of Castell Bryn Gwyn, consists today of two huge portal stones which from the road appear to be part of the hedge and adjacent gate. On arriving at the stones, the first reaction is always one of awe because these are two immense rocks that dwarf any guests who have braved the hazardous sludge, which acts as a form of endurance initiation before arriving at the site.

Standing stones on Anglesey are usually of blade appearance and are of a quite manageable size, but these two giant megaliths are different; they are huge and unique to the island. A repeating feature of British ancient sites is a phenomenon known as Diamonds and Lozenges or pairs of male and female stones. This can be found in abundance at Avebury, where an avenue of megaliths leading from the main stone circle is constructed using this principle. In fact the portal stones at

Bryn Gwyn Tre'r Dryw would not be out of place in the Avebury circles and avenue.

I realize that it is not polite to speak of a lady's vital statistics but our particular friend here, who is adorned with an eye-catching seam of rose quartz down her back, nearest to the hedge, has a body made up almost entirely of white quartz. She is a tall girl standing at 10 feet high and has a waist measurement of 22 feet. Miss Bryn Gwyn Tre'r Dryw could well be the sister of the main stone at the Duloe Stone Circle which sits south of Bodmin Moor in Cornwall and which also consists entirely of white quartz. The male stone, which has a body of granite, is taller than his partner and he stands at over 15 feet with a blade appearance with a width of only 15 inches at its widest point.

The question has to be whether this dinner party, male-then-female theme was a feature of the original stone circle, but regrettably the answer eludes us at this time, as it is extremely difficult to locate the position of the stones of the original circle, if this site did start life as a circle, as many experts now believe. When Henry Rowlands visited the site, he reported finding four stones *in situ* and from these he believed that they had been part of an arc, which would have produced a circle of around 40 feet in diameter.[7] Assuming the stones to have been of a similar size to the two surviving megaliths, the circle here would have been a magnificent site and one to rival any in Britain.

Burl reports[8] that the original stone circle was formerly surrounded by a wide bank and it certainly fills an interesting 15 minutes or so trying to spot the remains of any earthwork around the megaliths. Having visited the site in various

---

[7] Henry Rowlands, *Mona Antiqua Restaurata*, Kessinger Publishing, 2008.
[8] Aubrey Burl, *Stone Circles of Britain, Ireland and Brittany*, Pg.186, Yale University Press, 1995.

weather conditions, it would appear that you would get most success in locating any bank or ditch in damp conditions in the afternoon, when shadows appear to point out differences in height on either side of the field wall where the two stones stand.

A Return Visit ~ April 2008

I had thought that I had said all that was needed about the sites at Bryn Gwyn, until I revisited the area in April 2008. Not long before our visit the whole area had undergone a face lift of massive proportions. All the trees had been cut right back and the hedgerows had all but disappeared.

View of the stones and the henge from half way between the sites, April 2008

The result of all this radical landscaping activity was that for the first time in as many years that I had been visiting and speculating on the connectedness of these sites, all was revealed. Or at least a wonderful new clarity had been cast over the whole situation. It was now possible to view one site from the other and the overriding impression was that you were looking at not two separate sites, but one ceremonial landscape. The obstructions to sight had been removed, so as a group we searched out the best vantage point. This involved the use of two conveniently positioned stiles at either side of a farm track, which now bisects what must have been the original processional track way. From this height, all was revealed and it was remarkable just how close the sites actually are to each other. If a processional way had once existed between the two sites, it could have only been two or three hundred yards long at the most.

View of the stones and the henge from half way between the sites, April 2008

I have no idea how long it had been since this view had been possible but we felt extremely privileged to gain this new perspective.

4. Holy Penmon and Beaumaris
OS-114-631808

Penmon Church and Priory

So far our journey around the Isle of Anglesey has taken us along the southern section of the eastern coastal road, but now we are heading northeast in order to complete the final segment and to visit an area of immense importance to the growth and continuing history of this enchanting island.

Our destination is Holy Penmon, but in order to reach this peninsula we have to pass through the town of Beaumaris, which dates from the time of the construction of the last and largest of King Edward I's northern Welsh castles, in the early 1300s. The town, which overlooks both the Snowdon massif and the town of Bangor across the water, was strategically positioned to protect the island from marauders from across the Menai Strait and to take advantage of and control the ferry from the mainland and thus passing trade.

The construction of the castle and the foundation of the town came after a period of over 100 years of 'good times for the islands'. On the death of the Welsh King Gruffydd ap Cynan in 1170 AD, his son Owen Gwynedd succeeded and the construction of the earliest of Anglesey's fine stone churches dated from this time, indicating a period of great prosperity. Then in the last quarter of the thirteenth century the Gwynedd kings clashed with the English king, Edward I, resulting in two bloody and expensive wars where the Welsh king met his death in 1282. Gwynedd then passed to the English crown and Edward's administration set about dividing up the spoils in a 'fiscally creative manner' and in the process created the county of Anglesey.

Beaumaris Castle

As could have been expected, the overall reaction of the inhabitants of the new regions was not on the whole accepting of the new regime, and between 1294 and 1295 they tried for independence under Madog ap Llywelyn. The uprising was crushed and Edward ordered the construction of Beaumaris Castle and its supporting environs as a safeguard against future trouble.

The town's more recent history is one of tourism, which grew in no small measure as a result of the industrial revolution in the north of England and the demand for seaside resorts providing an annual bolt hole for factory workers fleeing the industrial sprawl for sun, sea and the beautiful Welsh countryside. To this end a ferry delivered a continuous cargo of guests from Liverpool and the Wirral. One of the main pubs on the high street is called the Liverpool Arms to this day.

Today visitors to the town of Beaumaris are greeted by amazing views over the strait to the mountainous mainland, but sadly as with many other British seaside resorts, you are left with the feeling of nostalgia, and that the best times the town had to offer have already been had by fun-seekers long gone. But Holy Penmon is to the north and it is in that direction we now turn our thoughts.

Leaving town by the final section of the northeast coast road as it weaves and narrows towards the Trwyn Du lighthouse, you find yourself at times almost on the water's edge, with the canoeists and kite flyers. The first sign you see of Holy Penmon are the remains of the Abbey and then, opposite the splendid Dovecot, a narrow path takes you past a fish pond, overgrown with a concentrated network of weeds. It is then only a couple of minutes before you find yourself in the wooded area which contains the remains of a sixth century Hermitage with an ancient sacred well as its centrepiece.

This was the one-time home of St Seiriol (known as St Seiriol the Fair), who settled on Anglesey in the second half of the sixth century with his friend St Cybi (known as St Cybi the Dark). The friends decided to make their homes and construct monasteries at opposite ends of the island. St Cybi's monastery eventually grew into the island's capital, today's town of Holyhead, and although this is about as far from St Seiriol's Penmon as he could possibly have managed, a story still remains about a regular meeting of the two early Christian brothers.

These meetings were said to have taken place every week in the town of Llanerchymedd, which lies near the centre of the island and would have been a strenuous walk from whichever direction the holy men approached the town. The choice of meeting place is particularly fitting, as it was at the meeting of three trackways, a place held to be sacred for thousands of years. Today the town is somewhat run down, although it still boasts a rather attractive church and the ancient trackways have grown into the meeting of the B5111 and the B5112.

Still, getting back to the story, St Cybi would set off from his home on Holyhead and would head east to meet his friend, thus having the rising sun in his face on his outward journey and heading west on his return journey, he would be walking towards the setting sun. St Seiriol, on the other hand, would be heading in the other direction to Llanerchymedd and would therefore have the sun on his back in both directions. This, it is said, is how the monks got their names: St Cybi the Dark because of the ample amount of sun he got on both legs of his weekly journey and St Seiriol the Fair because of the sun he did not get.

St Seiriol's Hermitage and Sacred Well

St Seiriol set up his hermitage and home in a holy place and next to an ancient well, which would have been a sacred place of meeting for thousands of years before the birth of the Christian religion. It seems probable that the Druids would also have known and respected this place, when the island was one of their main strongholds, from the last couple of centuries BC until they were eventually subdued by the Romans.

The well today is contained within an 18th century brick housing, consisting of three walls leaning on the same natural rocky face which had proved such a practical weather shelter for St Seiriol's Hermitage Cell, the stone remains of which can be seen to the left of the picture above. It is maybe slightly unfortunate that the shape of the well housing, whilst providing adequate shelter and a usable seat, somewhat restricts the flow of the stream, rendering the water undrinkable.

St Seiriol's Hermitage and Sacred Well

But this is a peaceful place and a place which lends itself to quiet meditation and reflection, especially, as you can see, on warm Sunday mornings when the site shows off its natural quality as a suntrap to its maximum potential. If you are not too careful a tour guide can lose his group to the tranquillity of such a place. It is at times like these, when it so easy to experience the very energy of Mother Earth, we can imagine our ancestors being similarly attracted and inspired to meet at places such as this long ago. The memories of religious ritual and ceremony over the millennia seem etched into the very landscape.

Relaxing at Penmon

It is places such as these that were the epicentre of an opportunity two thousand years ago to meld the collected wisdom of British spiritual thought with the new spiritual currents arriving from Jerusalem. Although this process did begin, it was unfortunately lost through the laying down of religious dogma. An amazing opportunity for the advancement of mankind was lost through this repression of human thought and the individual quest for spiritual advancement.

Penmon Priory or St Seiriol's Monastery

Penmon Priory

The present brick buildings, standing as if to keep a watchful eye over the sacred well, are dedicated to St Seiriol and are the result of rebuilding on the same spot since the time of his first settlement after the Romans left the island. Ancient Welsh records from Basingwerk Abbey indicate that the original monastery was approved by King Maelgwyn Fawr in the 540s AD. How much of the old British Celtic Christian belief system still existed at this time is debatable, but light has been shed on these otherwise Dark Ages, by contemporary writers such as St Gildas in 542 AD and by the early Christian historian Freculpus.[9]

Records show how evangelists came to Britain within the first few years after the death of Jesus. This was many years before

---

[9] Tim Wallace-Murphy, *The Knights of the Holy Grail: The Secret History of the Knights Templar*, Pg. 56, Watkins, 2007.

St Paul had devised his new religion on behalf of his Roman brethren. The original teachings of Jesus were well received and in many ways complemented and extended the existing spiritual teachings in the Britain of the time. The amalgamation of the two belief systems led to the creation of the Celtic Christian Church. This new worldview thrived in the heartlands of the Druids, such as Anglesey, with many Druids being priests of this new joint religion. St Columba is recorded to have said 'Jesus is my Druid'.[10] One cannot help but wonder where this peaceful and tolerant spiritual evolution would have led mankind had it been allowed to develop unchecked.

Anglesey's growing prosperity spread into the religious community and by the 10th century a fine wooden church was standing on the Penmon site, with two high crosses probably adorning each side of the entrance. These can still be seen on display in the church today. Unfortunately the good times were to be threatened as greedy Scandinavian eyes viewed the wealth of the British Isles from afar. The Viking invaders arrived on the shores of Anglesey in 971 AD, and in the ensuing raids the buildings at Penmon were burned to the ground. Records of habitation on the site then fell silent for around 170 years, until the reign of King Owain Gwynedd in the 1140s, when a stone church was constructed. Today, this forms the nave, central tower and south transept of the existing church, which has been turned into a rather chilly but extremely interesting museum. It is well worth putting some time aside to explore the gems the church has to offer; in particular look out for the ancient crosses and font from the same period, the dragon carving on the south doorway and the Sheela-na-gig in the south transept.

---

[10] Isabel Hill Elder, *Celt, Druid & Culdee*, The Covenant Publishing Co., 1938.

The next significant development took place in the reign of King Llywelyn the Great between 1220 and 1240, when monasteries in North Wales were restructured under the Augustinian Order. It was this period that saw the construction of the chancel and south transept of the existing church and the refectory, dormitory and cellars. The monastery buildings have been in ruins since Henry VIII dissolved them in 1537, when the lands passed to the local Bulkeley family, who used them as a deer park until the church underwent major reconstruction work in 1855.

There is a private toll road which leaves from the Penmon Priory car park and spans the short distance to Trwyn Penmon, or Penmon Point, were the bumpy puddled track runs out next to a wooden shack café. The car park here is strategically positioned to provide visitors with spectacular views of the lighthouse and Puffin Island in the near distance. This island, which was called Priestholm by the Vikings, is also known as Ynys Seiriol, or Seiriol's Island, and was once the location of a further monastic settlement founded by St Seiriol and is said to be the place of his burial.

If you are visiting Penmon, I recommend including this trip down to the Point in your plans, as the scenery is beautiful and you can look back to the distant mainland and try to pinpoint where you first spotted this place on your journey along the north coast of Wales. Anyway, you will probably have paid the road toll as part of your parking fee outside the monastery, so why not?

The Dovecot

Penmon Dovecot

Across the car-park from the ancient well is one of the best constructed and preserved dovecots in Britain. Originally built by Sir Richard Bulkeley around the year 1600, the Dovecot would have housed up to 1,000 nests, providing a continuous supply of eggs and fresh meat, invaluable during the winter months.

You enter by a miniature door to find that the square lower structure, covered with row upon row of nesting boxes, gives way to a cantilever domed roof containing a cupola, allowing the birds free access to enter and leave. A free-range farming arrangement provides an agreeable living space for the livestock, to which they readily return. How much more humane than hemming thousands of birds into the unhealthy environment we find in present-day battery farming.

The huge central pillar, which not surprisingly still remains in the centre of the tower, used to hold a revolving ladder, allowing ready access to the nesting boxes.

5. The Lligwy Region

Continuing on our traverse tour of the Island of Anglesey in a widdershins (anti-clockwise) direction, we have to head back from Penmon, through Beaumaris and then north to join the A5052, passing the beautiful Red Wharf Bay, until we reach the outskirts of the town of Moelfre, and the ancient Lligwy region. Here time has a way of appearing to distort. Although this area has been deserted for several hundred years, it had previously been occupied for millennia and it is the remaining monuments from three very different time periods (albeit with very similar masonry work) which causes this apparent temporal confusion.

As many sites such as this tend to be, Lligwy is situated on a hillside overlooking the most amazing sea views. Here you look out onto Lligwy Bay and the island of Ynys Dulas, dominated by its prominent tower.

Having left the usual parking bay, climbed the stile and read the obligatory Cadw[11] information sign, you discover the first of the Lligwy trio hiding behind the roadside hedge, inside a fenced-off pen. Lligwy Cromlech is the senior member of the family, dating back 4,500 – 5,000 years and is an unusual example of a so-called burial chamber. Then, a little further along the road and up a small rise into the forest, you suddenly encounter one of the most complete ancient settlements I have come across in Britain. Din Lligwy settlement was constructed up to 3,000 years after its older relation and yet the masonry work and type of stone used at both sites is so similar that they would appear at first sight to be contemporary. It is this enigmatic effect which creates the illusion of travelling through

---

[11] Cadw is the historic environment service of the Welsh Assembly Government. Many of Wales's historic sites and buildings are now in their care. 'Cadw' (pronounced cad-oo) is a Welsh word meaning 'to keep'.

time. The situation is only compounded when you come across the remains of the twelfth century chapel, Hen Capel Lligwy, on your way back down the hill to the road.

Lligwy Cromlech
OS-114-501860

Lligwy Cromlech

Of all the chambered tombs, dolmens, quoits, long barrows and cromlechs in Britain, the Lligwy Cromlech has to be ranked amongst the most unusual. This is a real crawling beastie of a site, with tiny legs under a gigantic protective shell. It sits pensively lowered onto a hollowed-out nest, ready to take off at a sprint if alarmed.

Lligwy's impressive capstone is 18 feet long and 15 feet wide and weighs around 25 ton. Close observation of the vertical edges reveals circular grooved columns which add to the beetle-like appearance of the structure, but which are probably the result of early masonry work. A common method of splitting stone into the desired proportions was to chisel out a straight line where you require a brake to be made, followed by the jamming of dry wooden stakes in to the newly revealed grooves. This would be followed by drenching the wooden stakes with copious amounts of water until they swell and eventually split the stone. This provides a rare insight into the skills of these stone masons from an advanced civilisation of up to 5,000 years ago. The work on the Unfinished Obelisk in Aswan, Egypt is a prime example of this method, as it shows the various stages in the process, which were left when the job was abandoned due to a hairline crack appearing in the main body of the structure.

An unusual feature of the Lligwy Cromlech is its distinctive hollowed-out interior, which has resulted in the ritual and burial area being below ground level, as opposed to the usual ground level floor surrounded by large megaliths. The construction process at Lligwy would appear to have been to dig out the so- called ritual area, or even carve it out of the rock shelf and then to arrange the supporting megaliths around the perimeter supported by a mound of curbstones. The curbstones would then provide a perfect ramp for the capstone to be pulled over the whole lot. Finally, the entire chamber would have been covered with smaller stones and earth.

At first glance, it appears as though the internal ritual area of the site is impenetrable, but if you persevere it is possible to gain entry and in fact the inner area turns out to be quite a lot bigger then you had imagined, due to the hollowed-out floor. The inner area has a peaceful atmosphere and to one side of the chamber there is even what appears to be a megalithic stone bed carved out of the bedrock. Sitting in this place reminds me of being a child and building dens in woodland near my home; this place would have been perfect. Of course today we are aware of the need to respect these ancient monuments built by our ancestors, and you still find signs here of recent rituals and offerings left by present day pagans.

The inner chamber at Lligwy Cromlech is at the centre of a particularly strange piece of folklore. The story is based around a fisherman who found himself running late on his way back from a fishing expedition. As night was coming in and he was still a long way from home, he was looking for shelter when he came across the cromlech and decided to take refuge. After finding his way under the capstone and into the chamber, he began to feel sleepy; maybe he found the stone carved bed and took a nap. He dreamt he was caught in a terrifying storm at sea, when he suddenly came across a beautiful maiden, who proceeded to rescue him and deliver him to dry land and safety. He was of course extremely grateful to the young maiden and asked what he could do in return for saving his life. At this point she turned into an ugly old witch who handed a snakeskin charm to the fisherman and told him to wash it once a year, or else! The moral of this tale can be left to the reader's imagination...

The origin of much of the folklore surrounding the ancient sites of Britain can be traced back to attempts to demonise anything which did not fit in snugly with the teachings of the Church. For example, the stones known as Long Meg and her daughters in Cumbria are said have been a coven of witches turned into stone for dancing on the Sabbath. A similar story is associated with the Merry Maidens Stone Circle at Land's End in Cornwall, while the name given to the magnificent Devil's Arrows megaliths in Yorkshire speaks for itself.

The earliest recorded excavation of Lligwy that I have been able to uncover took place a century ago, in 1909, when the remains of over 30 people were discovered in the main chamber. The discovery of fragments of beakers and pottery at the same time have led to the belief that the site was one of the

41

last monuments of its type to be in use in Britain, although it is possible that usage of the site could have changed over the millennia.

Din Lligwy Ancient Settlement
OS-114-496862

A Round Hut at Din Lligwy Settlement

There are some ancient sites which have the power to stir the imagination and the ancient settlement of Din Lligwy has an extraordinary ability to do this.

The path up to the site climbs slightly before running into a pleasant wooded area, with a carpet covering of natural garlic and then, as the path plateaus out, Din Lligwy greets you. It is a wonderful example of an ancient farming community, which was probably settled from the second half of the Iron Age, as early as 200 BC.

It is easy to visualise the inhabitants of this magnificent stone village, living contented lives in family units, surrounded by a perimeter wall of large limestone slabs, some 5 feet thick and filled with rubble and over 4 feet high. There is no reason to conclude that the wall had any military purpose, but it would certainly have protected the villagers from high sea winds and wild animals from the forest and would have stopped the livestock from wandering.

The hilltop position of all three of the Lligwy sites, with amazing sea views over the harbour, is a situation repeated over and over again throughout Britain, especially for chambered tombs and settlements. (The Huts on Holyhead Mountain, mentioned below, on the other side of the island, are another prime example.) This vantage point would have provided an ideal look-out so that it would have been almost impossible to arrive by sea without detection and the bay would have provided a ready supply of seafood throughout the year. All this is self evident, but we tend to forget the obvious fact that these sites are situated in places of great natural beauty, at which we marvel today. I feel sure that this must have at least been a factor when our ancestors decided where to have their homes and sacred sites. Today the view from the village is blocked by trees, but these have only grown up since the original inhabitants had long since moved on. It is highly likely that our ancestors would have sat watching the sun go down over the bay, from the Iron Age right through to the time they eventually abandoned the site, possibly to newer wooden structures in a community in the fields below.

The complex has a large open communal area and measures around half an acre in total. The buildings consist of two roundhouses and four rectangular warehouses, barns, workshops or livestock pens spaced out along the perimeter, with extra buildings formed by adjoining walls. Excavations have uncovered the remnants of various eras of habitation. For example, the largest rectangular building contained the remains of Iron Age smithy workings, such as metal slag, and smelting hearths with oak charcoal. One of the roundhouses was rich with coins from the Roman period, together with pottery, glass and a silver ingot, which would seem to indicate that this was the dwelling of the community leader. There is also a grove cut in the rock beside the entrance of this main roundhouse, which would seem to indicate a locking device, where a beam of wood could have been slid into position in order to secure the closed door.

The construction and use of the large stones of the area are so reminiscent of the Lligwy Cromlech that you find yourself pondering possible connections between the stonemasons who constructed the sites three thousand years apart. Were they related and part of continuing tribe with members living in the area for thousands of years? And did these people also build the nearby church at Hen Capel Lligwy?

Hen Capel Lligwy
OS-114-499864

Moving tour groups away from the peace of Din Lligwy always takes a little gentle persuasion, but eventually you have to pull yourself away and head back to the road. As you leave the forested area surrounding the old settlement, you notice the remains of an old church to the left and slightly down the sea facing hillside.

As you approach Hen Capel Lligwy you are again brought back to this feeling of moving through time. Although this fine old building was built around eight hundred years after the heyday of Din Lligwy and some 4,000 years after Lligwy

44

Hen Capel Lligwy

Cromlech, it is again constructed with similar stones and masonry work as its fellow sites. Work at Capel Lligwy probably followed the same stages of construction, from wood to brick, as Penmon Priory, a process of rebuilding which continued for at least the next four hundred years when a small chapel with a crypt was added to Hen Capel. It is interesting to go down into the tiny crypt today, although there is not really anything to see and the most interesting item in the chapel building is the ancient cross base which has just been left sitting forlornly in the corner.

The mid-thirteenth century was a period which could be called the post-Viking era, or a time when the Nordic immigrants were no longer raiding and had started to marry, settle and take up farming as a way of life. It was in these times that Capel Lligwy was constructed to serve a local community in times of relative peace and prosperity. It is probable that the settlement served by this Chapel of Ease consisted of wooden dwellings, which have long since vanished and that the church, as the only brick building affordable at the time, has been the only one to survive.

This could be the answer to our riddle of the disappearing inhabitants of Din Lligwy. Maybe in these times of relative peace, when societies and communities had the opportunity to become more organised, without the constant threat of pillage, they had decided to regroup in larger wooden houses beneath the present dwellings. Could it be that they eventually moved into the larger communities, which can now be seen still lower down the hillside and nearer to the sea? Could it be that the inhabitants of Moelfre are the ancestors of the stone masons who built the Lligwy monuments and who lived in the villages of Din Lligwy and the long disappeared settlement of Capel Lligwy?

Our time travelling experience has now taken us through 5,000 years from the Neolithic Cromlech, forward nearly 3,000 years to the Din Lligwy settlement and forward a further 1,000 years or so to Hen Capel Lligwy. It is amazing to think that it is only a further 800 years which connects us directly to these sites and when visiting Lligwy, I recommend taking a few quiet moments to reflect on this thought, whilst standing on the deserted hillside, which was continually occupied for at least 4,000 years, since man settled into a farming existence.

6. Parys Mountain Copper Mine
OS-114-442905

Parys Mountain

After leaving the Lligwy region, head northwest on the A5025 for around 10 minutes, before turning left at the roundabout just before Amlwch and you will see Parys Mountain ahead. You can take a drive round the mountain to view the results of the old mine workings and the entrance is one and a half miles up this road, on the left.

The sight of this much mined mountain with its heaps of copper, red, ochre and black coloured slag has to provoke mixed feelings. On the one hand, this is a place with a rich history going back 3,500 years, which allows us a fascinating look into our past and has also provided work for the local population for at least 500 years. On the other hand, to see a mountain destroyed in this way for its minerals is disturbing.

Taking the mountain trail, the vast expanse of diggings and the huge piles of discarded rocks, gives the appearance of a lunar landscape, or a volcanic landform. The impressive Montañas del Fuego (Fire Mountains) in Timanfaya National Park on the Canary Island of Lanzarote, is a prime example of a natural phenomena producing the same sort of excessively rugged effects leaving similar results to the scenes at Parys.

The use of copper heralded the end of the Stone Age and the first evidence of its use by the human population goes back at least 7,000 years. The word copper comes from the Roman 'Cyprium', the name for Cyprus, an important early source of the metal. Originally Copper would have been found in the form of ingots, lying in streams or in the walls of cliffs. This raw material would have easily been formed into tools, containers and jewellery, but it would not have been long before it was discovered that heating the metal would have a 'tempering' effect, producing a much harder and sturdy final product. The side effects of this process produce some decorative elements which would make colourful jewellery. Tempering would have lead to the 'smelting' process, which involves heating the raw materials at the much higher temperature of over 1,084 degrees, in order to remove the pure copper from unwanted minerals. Smelting produces a temporarily liquid form, which allows the mixing of other metals to produce an alloy and it was the amalgamation of copper with tin which led to the advent of the Bronze Age. It took a further 4,000 years of development before the mixing of copper and zinc produced brass around 600 BC.

It is probable that mining on Parys Mountain began by digging down into visible copper deposits, producing 'Bell pits', which eventually collapsed revealing oak charcoal. Radio carbon dating of these deposits indicates that mining had been taking place on the mountain at least as early as 3,500 BC and probably earlier, around the same time as at the other two Welsh mines at Llandudno and Cwmystwyth were beginning production. A later development would have been to pile logs against rock walls and setting fire to them in order to create heat, before quickly cooling them with water to crack the rock to reveal the more hard-to-reach copper deposits.

Mining on the mountain carried on through the Roman occupation and it is thought that the fort at Caer Gybi was built to protect the metals before they were exported to Rome and around the empire. After the Romans left, mining continued in a small way, but it was not until the late 17th century that any significant output was reached.

Up until the early 15th century the mountain was called Mynydd Trysglwyn, which translates as something like, 'hillside covered with a thick grove of rough trees covered with a scaly lichen grove'. Then, in 1404, the mountain was given to Robert Parys by King Henry IV, as a base for the collection of taxes from anti-royalist dissenters who had been on the side of Owain Glyndwr in a recent uprising. No mining took place at this time and it was not until the introduction of new technologies and uses for metals that production began in earnest in the 1690s; this soared to an all time high by the end of the 18th century, when Welsh mines were the biggest in the world.

Over the years, Parys Mountain has had a dramatic effect on the population of Anglesey, and the Amlwch area in particular, as fluctuations in output contributed to cycles of prosperity then impoverishment. In the 1840s, the mine appeared to have dried up and production hit an all time low; the resulting economic slump led to widespread malnutrition among the local populace, many of whom contracted Typhus fever as a consequence.

Love it or hate it, it is beyond doubt that this mountain overlooking Amlwch has been interwoven in the affairs of the people of the area for many thousands of years and today continues to do so as a tourist attraction, bringing people into the surrounding towns and villages. However, it may still have a future as a mine: new hope for the miners restarting work emerged in 2008, when the Anglesey Mining Company began talks with Western Metals of Australia to win investment in the plant. It seems there is life yet left in Parys Mountain, and its long story may be far from over.

7. Bodewryd Standing Stone
OS-114-406902

The Bodewryd Standing Stone

From Parys Mountain, continue south along the B5111 and take the right turn after Rhosybol and right again at Rhosgoch. Then right at the crossroads, called The Four Crosses, and keep a keen eye on the hedgerow to your right until you see the Bodewryd Stone in the centre of the field. A little further down the road you will find a convenient lay-by with a gate into a field of unusually neat grass.

Solitary standing stones are scattered around Anglesey and are too numerous to cover in this book, so I have selected the Bodewryd Stone as I think it is one of the best examples and well worth a visit.

You can easily see the stone from the gate at the lay-bay, standing around 100 yards away in the centre of the field. As you approach Bodewryd, it appears like a slender spike pointing 12 feet into up into the air, but as you get nearer you realise that you have been looking at the narrow edge of the stone. In fact it has a width of around 5 feet and is reminiscent of the blade stone at Bryn Gwyn Tre'r Dryw. The lichens have found a great home on the Bodewryd Stone and they give it an interesting assortment of purples, yellows and light greens.

The stone gets its name from the Bodewryd estate, on which it stands, but it also has two other Welsh names, Carreglefn, which translates as the 'Smooth Stone' and Maen Pres, 'the Brass Stone'. This second name relates to the interesting folklore stories, which tell of how treasure is buried around the stone and that its shadow will point out the location at a certain time on a particular day every year. If you solve this problem by finding an inscription on the stone, you will discover the booty buried in a brass container. It is also said that if you read the inscription out loud, then the stone will oblige by moving to one side and revealing the treasure.

8. Mein Hirion Standing Stones
OS-114-364917

Mein Hirion Standing Stones

From the Bodewryd Stone, go back to the Four Crosses crossroads and turn left towards Amlwch. Take the A5025 from the town towards Cemaes and follow the sign to the village of Llanfechell, which lies beneath the intriguing three standing stone arrangement of Mein Hirion.

It is not an easy thing to locate this fine trio and on the first couple of visits I approached the site from totally the wrong direction and found myself directing my Megalithic Travellers over an assault course involving a precarious balancing act across a small but boggy area. I have since located a much safer and dryer path, which leads from a farm on the road from Cemaes Bay into Llanfechell, over a couple of relatively easy stiles and across two or three fields and there you are overlooking the town and with panoramic, 360 degree views over land and far out to sea.

A boggy retreat from Mein Hirion

The Mein Hirion stones stand out as special and indeed they do have a unique formation and an electric feel to them, sitting as they do in a wonderful elevated position, high above the nearby villages and homesteads. This place excites the imagination: is it the centre of an ancient trig directional system of connecting sites? If so, where are the others? Standing within the stones and looking around, it is not easy to locate any obvious continuation of a network or ley line system. Was this a holy place, where our ancestors would meet to connect with their deity and each other? To these questions we can only speculate. Time has washed any memories away, for now at least. But standing here amongst these superlative megaliths, none of this really matters.

A three stone formation is highly unusual, but Mein Hirion's blade-like stones associate it with other similar sites. They are particular reminiscent of two pairs of twin standing stones, the Penrhos Feilw on Anglesey's Holy Island and the Giant's Grave standing on the southern coast of Cumbria, beneath Swinside stone circle and the Black Combe (Mother) Mountain. It is said that Mein Hirion may have been part of a larger site, maybe a stone circle, but I do not think so. Not only because of the total lack of anything resembling megalithic remains in the vicinity, but also perhaps more importantly, this place just feels complete.

9. Presaddfed Chambered Tomb
OS-114-347808

Preʃaddfed Chambered Tomb

After leaving Cemaes Bay and travelling anti-clockwise along the A5025 for around thirteen miles, passing small towns with similar sounding names such as, Llanrhyddlad, Llanfaethlu and Llanfechell, a left turn onto the B5109 at Llanynghenedl takes you through Bodedern to the Presaddfed Estate. The chambered tomb sits within the estate, just past the lodge house in the centre of a large green field to the left. On entering the field through the kissing gate, you have the impression of a site which, unusually, is dwarfed by the size of the field, with its surrounding patchwork of woodland. I am sure that Presaddfed would have been spectacular and dominant in its day, but in its present state and setting, it is hard to imagine.

It is low ground here and at certain times of the year, and after heavy rain, the nearby Llyn (lake) Llywenan encroaches into the Presaddfed field and it can get quiet wet underfoot. Boots are highly recommended here!

Although chambered tombs are numerous on Anglesey, they all have their own distinctive characteristics and Presaddfed is no exception. At first sight it appears as two separate chambers standing close together and in many ways this is exactly what it is, except that the two chambers are part of the same site. This, like its sister site Trefignath a few miles to the west, is a dolmen with multiple chambers.

As you draw nearer and things start to take shape, you begin to realise that this whole place is occupied by some ever so slightly aggressive inhabitants, who are none to keen to have their privacy and personal space invaded. These woolly members of the local sheep population are not the first locals to claim squatter's rights here. It is said that a homeless family from one of the nearby towns moved into the main chamber sometime in the 18th Century after being evicted by a harsh landlord.

The covering of curbstones at Presaddfed has completely disappeared and the site, being in a poor state of repair, has a somewhat dilapidated appearance. The southernmost chamber has received some careful first aid at some point, in the form of a well positioned wooden splint which, whilst adding nothing to the site's overall aesthetics, has enabled the chamber to remain to some extent complete. Its partner, lying seven feet away to the north, has not been so lucky: its wonderfully heart-shaped cap stone lays sadly collapsed on top of one of its upright supporting stones. There has never been access between the two chambers and today it is not clear in which direction the original entrance faced.

10. Holyhead and the Holy Isle

Reversing your route from Presaddfed back to the Llanynghenedl and turning left onto the A5025, you are less than three miles from Anglesey's very own Holy Island. A mile before you arrive on the island you are faced with a choice of two bridge crossings and three roads. The A5025 becomes the B4545 and the minor route and the A5, A55 and the railway take a second bridge which forms the trunk route directly into the main town of Holyhead. For our purposes this will be the direction of choice as we are in search of St Cybi, the clerical friend of St Seiriol, whom we met earlier at Holy Penmon.

Entering Holy Island

Holyhead is not one of the quaint seaside fishing harbours or deserted villages we have been used to on our journey so far; its close proximity to Ireland has transformed the town to a busy modern working port, with trains, buses and ferries continually arriving and departing. This is a relatively large town with hotels and B&Bs lining the streets, providing a slightly shabby appearance, which is only partially rectified by the views from the promenade and Beach Road. From here you can look out at the boats and yachts, moored on the still waters before the breakwater and then due north out over Holyhead Bay and the open seas beyond.

St Cybi's Church and Caer Gybi Roman Fort

St Cybi's Church

The church of St Cybi stands at the heart of Holyhead and is still very much a place of worship. Seeking protection within a three walled Roman harbour fort, it is somewhat of an enigmatic site, but a look into our holy man's history provides some insight into why he may have sought to build his place of sanctuary within such a place of security. It is somewhat ironic that this sentiment has passed down through the generations, as a visit to the church and fort in these days of vandalism and little deference to religious authority, reveals strengthened wire frames and grids over the windows.

St Cybi was born a Cornishman in Callington near Plymouth in 480 AD, the son of the Chieftain, Selyf and great grandson of Cystennin Gorneu, considered in Welsh history to be the grandfather of King Arthur. His connection with the legend does not end there as his mother Gwen was related to Vortigern, who met Merlin whilst experiencing problems constructing his fort on the mountain Dinas Emrys, near Beddgelert in Gwynedd. St Cybi relinquished the opportunity of royalty by succeeding his father and instead followed his first cousin, St David the patron saint of Wales, to become a Christian monk.

He left his homelands and travelled with a small group of followers, spreading the Word and founding churches. One such is St Cuby's church near Liskeard which stands across the road from a most amazing quartz stone circle, already 2,500 years old when the early church was being planned. After a time in Wales, he quarrelled with King Edelig and moved to Ireland with St David and settled on Arran Island in Galway Bay. Their four year long furlough ended when he and his followers had to leave this remote outpost after an outlandish argument with the head Irish monk, Crubthir Fintan, over a cow. This pattern continued until Maelgwn, King of Gwynedd, eventually granted them the abandoned fort at Pentre Gwyddel, which eventually became known as Caer Gybi and then Holyhead.

Fort wall at Caer Gybi

The fort is an extremely unusual construction, consisting of three walled sides, with the fourth overlooking the sea which lies at the bottom of a steep embankment. Today the view from the church through the open segment takes in the port and the massive Catamaran-hulled fast ferry to Dublin. In the late 4th century the Romans built the fortification for the purpose of defending the outskirts of their territory from Irish invaders, in the troubled years towards the end of the empire, when it would have looked out onto a beach and quay. The fort was an outpost of Deva, or Chester, and would have been manned by the Valeria Victrix, the 20th Legion, who had a secondary garrison at Segontium in Caernarfon.

St Cybi settled at Caer Gybi in 540 AD and built a monastic settlement which became known as 'Clas' and he remained there until his death in 554 AD, at the age of 84. The monastery continued until the reformation in the 16th century, but his cult following lives on to this day in the churches he formed. In his time Cybi was known as a highly educated and respected cleric in favour of the Celtic church in the years before the Synod of Whitby in 664 AD. It was at this fateful gathering that the Roman Church finally overthrew its rival, creating one Christian church under the dogma decided upon at the Council of Nicaea in 325 AD.

After being ransacked in 961 AD by Viking raiders led by Iron Knee and Sitric the Silken Beard, the church of St Cybi was rebuilt. The present Chancel is built upon 13th century foundations and major work has been carried out at various times down the years. In more recent times some beautiful stained glass windows have been added, including an east window in 1879 by Charles Eamer Kempe.

Holyhead Mountain Settlement or Ty Mawr Hut Circles
OS-114-212820

A couple of miles to the west of Holyhead stands a mountain of the same name. Rising to a height of 722 feet, it provides a craggy backdrop and a welcome invitation to the freedom of the countryside, for anyone who has spent a night in the town. The far slopes of the mountain drop steeply to the sea, but a minor road to the east leads you to the South Stack lighthouse and RSPB reserve, a major Welsh tourist attraction. The seascapes from South Stack are truly breathtaking and I have taken parties to the vast areas of heather covering the mountainside on sunny days, when it is generally agreed that nowhere in the world could beat the stunning views.

But we are here to visit something generally overlooked by the multitudes of holiday makers who are inclined to stay on the seaward side on the road. We are here to call in at an ancient settlement, whose inhabitants moved on over 1,500 years ago, around the time St Cybi was settling over the other side of the mountain.

When taking tours here, I have noticed an initial reluctance in the group to cross the road from the RSPB Reserve car park, as the natural tendency is to head in the direction of the sea and the spectacular cliffs. I have to promise time to wander after we have visited the site, although this is not always required as the hut settlements, once discovered, are not easily abandoned. The kissing gate creaks as if to announce your approach to the long gone residents, but your first impressions are of a hillside covered with fern and heather and not much else. The colours vary depending on the time of the year, from the green shoots of spring, to the vibrant purples and yellows of summer and then, as Mother Earth turns her wheel of the year towards autumn, the beautiful oranges and coppers, making ready for next year's new beginnings.

Holyhead Mountain Hut

You make your way up a gently sloping path between the vegetation and after a couple of minutes you encounter the first hut, 20 feet in diameter with thick, well defined low walls cut out of the undergrowth and its stone sink embedded into the ground. Your imagination immediately comes into play: what were these people like, did they live peaceful lives, did they have worries about invasion or food shortage, how many lived in the place? So many questions are evoked. Orthodox writings covering such subjects point to the abundance of seafood and the high vantage point providing an early warning system in case of attack.

Of course, this is all true and there is evidence that the inhabitants of Holyhead Mountain ate food gathered from the sea and seem to have had a fondness for limpets. They were also farmers and ground wheat on the stones that are still present in some of the huts. But these were human beings, and they must have looked out over the sea and marvelled at the views, much as we do thousands of years later.

Having found your first round hut, you soon find a rectangular storage cupboard and then you find another and another hiding, until you are nearly on top of them. There are over 20 of these preserved structures, but there must have been many more when the site was at its peak population. Inhabitation began here at least 4,000 years ago and probably much earlier and continued through the Bronze Age, the Iron Age and eventually ended in the 6th century AD. Did the population eventually drift over the mountain nearer to Caer Gybi, where the centre of activity had started to focus, now that the famous monk St Cybi had built the new monastery?

Penrhos Feilw Standing Stones
OS-114-227809

Leaving South Stack by the narrow winding coastal road in the direction of Treardurr Bay, in less than five minutes you come across a left turn. Around 100 yards up Plas Road, as this single lane track is called, you reach a farmhouse on the left. In the field behind the house are two standing stones, appearing at first glance as megalithic goal posts. The Penrhos Feilw Standing Stones are in a wonderful setting with Holyhead Mountain to the north, sea views over the bay of Abraham's Bosom to the west and to the south in the distance, the hills on the Llynn Peninsula, on the far side of Caernarfon Bay, which on a clear day, appear a lot closer than they really are.

Penrhos Feilw Standing Stones

The stones stand some 10 feet above the ground and 10 feet apart and have a blade-like appearance rising to a rounded point. The upper portions are covered with the type of lichen used by model railway enthusiasts as miniature trees and bushes.

Sites like these provoke conversation, questions and speculation. Comparison can be made with such similar sites as the pair of standing stones on the South Cumbria coast called the Giant's Grave and the triple stones of Mein Hirion near Llanfechell (discussed above). Is it possible that this site was once part of a much larger sacred landscape, such as can be found on Machrie Moor on the Isle of Arran or Kilmartin Glen on the Kintyre Peninsula? The answer would have to be yes, as this is a large area with evidence of settlements not far away on the mountainside and a chambered tomb less than a mile away.

Could these two proud megaliths mark out an ancient trackway, or even a religious processional way? Do they indicate that Holyhead Mountain was once considered a holy place in times long ago to the people who once inhabited this holy island?

Trefignath Chambered Cairn
OS-114-258806

Trefignath Chambered Cairn

The coastal road south from Penrhos Feilw passes the rocky and secluded bays of Porth Dafarch and Porth y post before arriving at the popular holiday destination of Treardurr Bay. The stunning views and golden beaches of this stretch of coastline attract tens of thousands of visitors every year, especially those interested in water-sports. You then pass through the small busy holiday town of Treardurr, with its large hotels and pass straight across the B4545, staying on the minor narrow road back towards Holyhead.

Trefignath appears on the right about a mile further on, but it sits in an unfortunate position, just beneath the A55 expressway. At the time of writing this whole plateau area was undergoing development on a massive scale and it is probable that any future site visits to Trefignath will reveal roads and buildings encroaching nearer and nearer to the site.

It is difficult to imagine a less appealing backdrop to Holy Isle's grand plateau, which must have once been a mighty and awesome place. Firstly there is the unsightly aluminium works to contend with and then the A55, which was added as an extra road across the island, to ease pressure on the existing A5.

It is a good idea to visit Trefignath Chambered Tomb on the same day as Presaddfed, as the two sites are not only relatively close to each other, but are also of similar design. A comparison of the two sites is interesting and provides a better understanding of, and insight into, them both.

Trefignath was constructed on an impressive outcrop of rock, a natural foundation which may have been in use long before the time of these chambers. There are continuing theories that mankind would have had places of meeting during the millennia they spent as wandering hunter-gatherers. They would have met at places considered sacred to the wandering tribes, such as waterfalls, springs, wells, the meeting of three trackways and rocky outcrops such as these.

There has been further evidence of earlier inhabitation at the Trefignath site since 1977. As the world was listening to the Bee Gees' *Staying Alive*, Trefignath was coming alive again after around 4,500 years, as the first excavations at the site were uncovering pottery and stone and flint tools from a layer below the present site's construction.

During a further two years of excavation, three clearly defined chambers were divested of their original covering mound of curbstones and earth and laid bare for all to see. Unusually for Anglesey chambers, Trefignath has managed to retain its collection of curbstones and these can still be seen surrounding the site, leaving the observer the task of rebuilding the mound to its original condition in the mind's eye.

Continual usage usually means continual stages of construction, as we have witnessed at such sites as Bryn Celli Ddu (above), and most prominently at Stonehenge on the Wiltshire Plains. The Trefignath cairns were constructed and used over a period of some 1,500 years, from around 3800 BC until they were finally sealed and abandoned around 2300 BC.

The earliest chamber to be constructed was a stone box formation to the westerly end of the site, with two huge seven feet long stone slabs forming the main chambers walls. The central chamber was added later, but unfortunately this one has fared less well over time and has all but collapsed, leaving only one portal stone and one lone rear supporting stone standing, with a further side stone and the fractured capstone lying nearby.

The final chamber, which stands to the far east of the site, is by far the best preserved, with its inner area probably appearing today more or less as it did at its time of construction, except with a little help from a brick support to the north-east of the chamber. This piece of protective safety equipment is of a type inserted into Cadw-protected monuments around the island and at Trefignath at least the plinth does not detract greatly from the aesthetic properties of the site. Entering this magnificent eastern chamber takes you between two stately looking portal stones, each standing over six feet tall. The inner chamber consists of a wall of five megaliths, supporting two huge capstones.

Ty Mawr Standing Stone
OS-114-254809

The Ty Mawr Standing Stone

The mighty Ty Mawr stone is just a couple of hundred yards due north-west from Trefignath and has to be part a complex of ancient sites with the chambered cairns at its hub. Unfortunately, this part of Holy Island has been developed, if that is the right word, to the point where the wonderful stone monuments, which would have adorned this place, now sit uneasily between the factories, supermarkets and expressways.

To reach the stone is an easy matter of following the new and seemingly pointless road from Trefignath in the direction of Holyhead. On the many occasions I have visited the ancient sites here I have never seen anyone use this road, but maybe it is part of a greater plan and that locals know something I don't; we can only wait and see what the town planners have in store for this once holy landscape. Ty Mawr stands almost despondently in a fenced-off field to the right, but thankfully a gate has been fitted which allows access to the stone. This must mean that someone somewhere has the job of looking out for the ancient sites of the area and that, at least, can only be a good thing.

Ty Mawr herself is a proud uneven blade-style monolith standing over 9 feet tall, with a broad base and an upper section tapering off to a half rounded, half flattened point. The stone has the shape of the type of earth Goddess found in the temples of Malta, but she does not seem to be at one with her surroundings here, now that the bulldozers have had their way!

Rhoscolyn Burial Chamber
OS-114-271752

Take the B4545 south out of Trearddur for a couple of minutes before taking a right turn onto the side road towards Rhoscolyn, where an extremely narrow road takes you down to Borthwen beach and a car park with a slipway leading into the shallow bay. The sloping beach invites you to linger and take in the idyllic setting with a backdrop of dunes and the mountains on the mainland in the distance, visible through the narrow bay entrance lined with remote islands.

The burial chamber is next to a large house and is reached by climbing over a stile on the wall of the slipway. The site fits the usual characteristics of a Welsh cromlech: it is in a beautiful setting overlooking the sea, with four supporting megalithic walls and a huge capstone. The design is nearly perfectly symmetrical and is set in a concrete foundation but it just does not feel quite right and the stage looks a little *too* set.

Rhoscolyn Burial Chamber

The view from Borthwen Beach

The capstone is neatly resting on all four of the upright stones in a way that is extremely rare as most tombs of this sort have shifted over the millennia and are usually unstable and resting limited points of contact. The Anglesey Information website[12] records that the chamber was standing in the 1940s, but before that its genuineness is not certain. The question of Rhoscolyn's authenticity is an interesting one and a good reason for a visit in itself. Was the chamber built as a folly by the then owners of the neighbouring house, or is it a *bona fide* Neolithic Chamber, re-built in a haphazard way by a Victorian antiquarian?

---

[12] www.anglesey.info

11. Llyn Cerrig Bach
OS-114-305766

Leaving Holy Island by the A5, turn right at the roundabout towards RAF Valley, three miles after crossing the bridge. This road takes you through an RAF housing estate, with lines of standard drab service houses, before the waters of Llyn Penrhyn open up on the right and you see the airstrip of RAF Valley ahead. It is at this point that the paranoid amongst us start to wonder about the armed guards watching from the entrance barriers, but be brave and continue towards the runway in spite of this imagined threat. On reaching the airstrip, the road is forced to take a sharp right bend and the Cadw boards are to be found on the right-hand verge few hundred yards further on.

Llyn Cerrig Bach

The lake is through the long grasses just past the boards. It is a small tarn hidden behind bulrushes that edge onto the road; on the far side, flat marshlands stretch off into the distance. There is a strange melancholy feeling about the place and it must have been very different when the area was so venerated two thousand years ago. It is an almost impossible task to imagine that Llyn Cerrig Bach used to be so significant and holy a place to ancients and Druids alike.

It was in 1942, as the RAF runway was being enlarged as part of the war effort to receive the massive American 17-ton Flying Fortresses, that one of the most important Celtic hoards in Europe was discovered. Llyn Cerrig Bach, or the 'Lake of the small stones', had reduced over time from a fine lake to a boggy area with one large island. It was here that probably hundreds of artefacts had been thrown in ceremonies from around 200 BC up to a dozen or so years before the Roman invasion of 60 AD.

The depositing of valuable gifts as offerings to the Deities at such places was a widespread tradition, which has been reflected in legends such as the sword Excalibur and the Lady of the Lake and can still be seen today in the practice of throwing coins into wells. The treasure trove recovered at Llyn Cerrig Bach included over 150 ornaments, tools and weapons from the Celtic and Iron Age periods, such as slave-chains, trumpets, cauldrons, chariot fittings, swords, shields, spear-heads, blacksmiths' tools, elaborately decorated plaques and bracelets. Many of the artefacts were of high quality metalwork and from as far afield as the north-west and south-east of England and Ireland, which would suggest that the island had been considered a holy place and a place of pilgrimage.

Bizarrely, the valuable hoard was discovered when a lorry got stuck in the bog, whilst dredging the area to extend the runway. One of the local workers, by the name of William

Roberts, fixed a chain he had found in the mud to a tractor to allow them to tow the truck clear. The chain was used throughout the day to remove vehicles from the quagmire until an engineer from the RAF base examined it and recognised that there was more to it than just a piece of old farming equipment left many years ago, as had originally been thought. He called in Sir Cyril Fox from the National Museum of Wales in Cardiff who identified the chain as a 2,100 year old 'gang chain' of around 10 feet in length with loops for holding human ankles and necks. He immediately postponed work on the runway whilst he recovered as many of the ancient relics as possible and removed them to the National Museum in Cardiff, where they still remain.

The weapons gathered around Llyn Cerrig Bach have changed over the thousands of years since our ancestors left their swords and shields in the lake. More recently these have been replaced by a whole row of BAE Hawk T1 Trainer jets, each worth £18 million and complete with tactical weapons training facilities. We have evolved into a species that can now kill in the thousands at the push of a button.

12. Ty Newydd Burial Chamber
OS-114-345738

Ty Newydd Burial Chamber

Continuing along the A5, turn left onto the A4080 after around five miles and then right at Llanfaelog and Ty Newydd is tucked away in the corner of a field on the right of the road off a left hand bend. The countryside around the Llanfaelog area is flat and fertile and you can see for miles from the north round to the west and the mountains of the Snowdonia range beyond the overgrown hedges to the south and east. The field has had different crops every year and the picture above was taken just after the harvest. A series of small bollards at the edge of the field are nothing to do with the original shape of the site, but in fact mark out the edge of the protected area.

Ty Newydd started life as a typical chambered tomb and its covering of curbstones survived until the 19th century. An excavation which took place in 1936 found some beaker pottery fragments and a Bronze Age flint, but nothing of any great significance as far as putting a definitive date on the site. It could have been this uninvited invasion that heralded the end for this once magnificent monument, which has probably stood here for up to 5,000 years. Excavations at this time appear to have been little more than grave robberies, showing little if any respect for the site and making no attempt at reconstruction, or putting things back in the state they were in before work started.

In more recent years Ty Newydd has had an ill-fated history. Without its protective covering it nearly collapsed at one point and had to be propped up with two unfortunate square brick supports. This essential repair has seriously detracted from the aesthetic value of the site, but at least a visitor can still get some idea as to the size and shape of the tomb. At the same time as the supports were fitted, the massive capstone, of 12 feet by 5 feet, suffered a fracture and was itself in need of the additional support, just to keep it from breaking into two pieces.

I will still call in and visit this once great chambered cairn as it has kept its charm and regal atmosphere in the face of adversity. The ambience at Ty Newydd is tranquil and relaxing, especially on a sunny day, and it is one of those sites where people enjoy spending a little time to sit and meditate and to take the whole experience in.

13. Barclodiad y Gawres Burial Chamber
OS-114-329707

Leaving the Ty Newydd Burial Chamber by the A4080 and heading towards the coast, you pass through the village of Llanfaelog and then before you know it, the spectacular sight of Porth Trecastell opens up on your right. Overlooking the bay there is the type of small car park that is always covered with a veneer of sand, but provides views magnificent and an ever-present ice-cream van.

Barclodiad y Gawres Burial Chamber

There is nothing better than taking a few moments to enjoy a cornet, whilst soaking in the atmosphere of the cove. Trecastell is a small box inlet of the type the Vikings called 'Voes'. There are many of these in lands with a history of Norse occupation, such as the Shetlands. The high cliff walls around the bay would provide protection for longboats, pulled well up onto the shallow sandy beaches. Here in Anglesey the banks are grassy above the tidal rock strata and the narrow seaward entrance forces a constant ripple of waves to leave a residue of salty foam on the beach.

An Iron Age promontory fort once stood strategically positioned on the cliff to the left, although there is very little left to indicate its presence today except some low remaining earthworks. Gazing out to sea, the fort's primary function would have been to act as an early warning system against invaders, but it is probable that markets and other gatherings would have been held here and that people would have used it as a place of meeting.

From the car park you can make out a raised grassy dome on the high peninsula to the right, opposite the cliff with the fort. This is Barclodiad y Gawres (pronounced 'Barclod-Eye-Add Ub Gowrez') Burial Chamber, one of the most important ancient sites in Wales. The path up to the site starts in a narrow deep sandy rut and takes a steady but slight climb, which eventually opens up to a wide grass plateau after about 5 minutes.

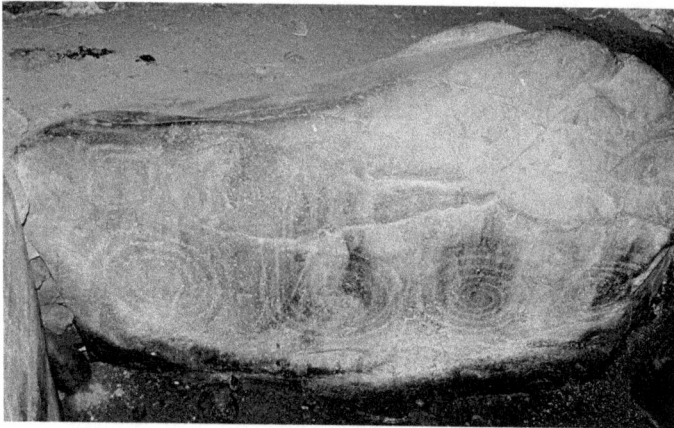

Spiral Carved Stone at Barclodiad y Gawres

Arriving at the site, it appears to be another Bryn Celli Ddu, with a completed symmetrical dome covering an inner chamber. Unfortunately, this shell turns out to be a concrete structure, built over the site in order to protect the remains of the tomb and the fine collection of five carved standing stones housed in the gloomy dark. The north facing brick built entrance has been blocked by a gated iron fence, so it is important to make arrangements to collect the key before your visit.

This used to be done by merely calling at a nearby hardware store and exchanging a five pound deposit for a key and a torch. But at the time of writing this procedure is under review, after an extremely unfortunate incident in 2008, when a supervised school party vandalised the stones with spray paint.

This mindless act of destruction inflicted on a priceless 5,000 year old monument not only cost many thousands of pounds to rectify, but makes you wonder what is being taught in schools about our heritage. Maybe a section in the curriculum covering the thousands of years of civilised society that existed in Britain before the Roman invasion might be a worthwhile addition.

Entering the dark inner chamber is an eerie experience when you first catch sight of the large bulky shapes lurking in the gloom, like so many ghostly figures. But soon you become accustomed to the light and begin to make out firstly the standing stones and capstone of the chambered tomb, then the superb carvings in the form of spirals, chevrons and lozenges. This has to be the finest collection of rock art in Britain, resembling many examples to be found in the passage graves of the Carnac area of Brittany in Northern France.

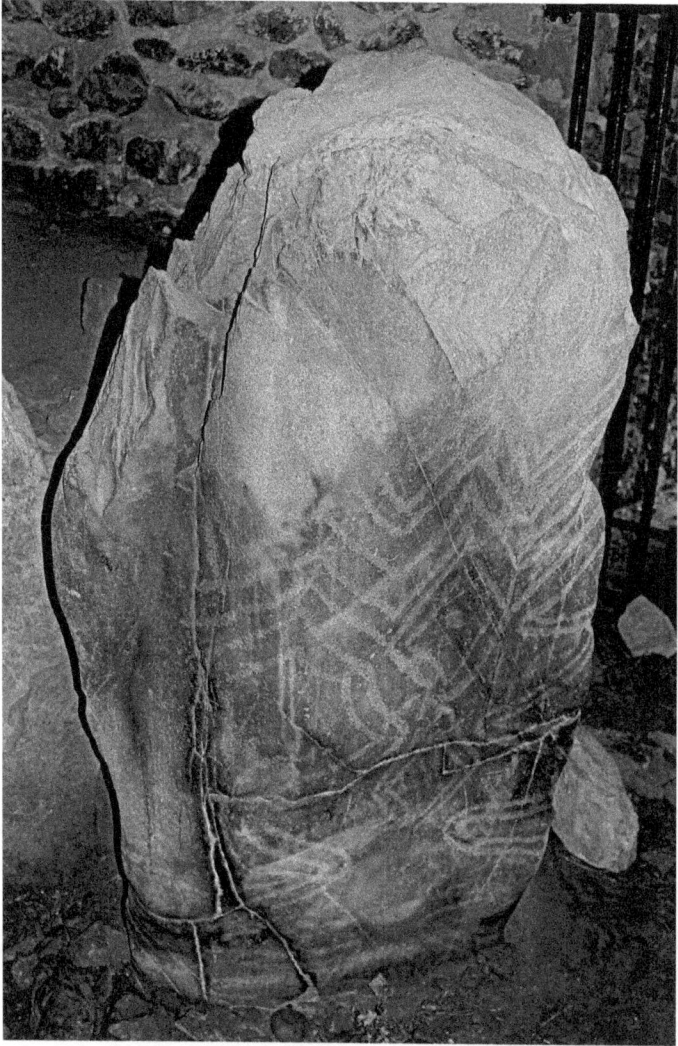

Chevron and Lozenge Carved Stone at Barclodiad y Gawres

The original layout of Barclodiad y Gawres was reminiscent of many chambered tombs such as West Kennet Long Barrow in Wiltshire, Capel Garmon, near Betws y Coed in Conwy and the Tomb of the Eagles on South Ronaldsay in the Orkney Islands. The main passage is north-facing and 23 feet in length, ending in three main chambers in a cross formation at the southern end, with two sub-chambers in the western partition. An excavation in 1952/53 discovered cremated human remains and bits of bone.

The Oriel Ynys Môn museum in Llangefni periodically exhibits a full scale model of Barclodiad y Gawres in its History Gallery and if you are lucky enough to see this, it is extremely helpful in aiding the imagination to form a full impression of the site. The museum also displays a cooking fire scene which has been created around the actual archaeological finds from the tomb, including the remains of an ancient fire with food remnants mixed amongst the ashes. The food ingredients appear to have been for a Neolithic stew and include whiting, eel, frog, Natterjack toad, grass snake, mouse and hare. The remains were covered with limpet shells and small pebbles. From this evidence it would appear that our ancestors enjoyed a high quality and nutritious diet of fresh food from both land and sea.

Barclodiad y Gawres translates as the Giantess's Apronful, which is a recurring name for ancient sites throughout Europe, such as the magnificent Ggantija Temple on the Maltese island of Gozo. Our Anglesey site though has an absorbing piece of folklore attached to it, which reads like an enthralling fairy-tale.

As the story goes, there were once a couple of married giants who were making their way to Anglesey. The tale does not say where they came from, but only that it was their intention to build a house and settle on the island. To help them with their task they had loaded themselves up with plenty of stones: the husband carried two large boulders to act as doorposts, while his wife had a whole stash of smaller stones secreted in her apron. After walking many a mile, they encountered an old cobbler approaching from the opposite direction, in a place called Bwlch y Ddeufaen (The Pass of the Two Stones). As they were beginning to get a bit weary, they asked the cobbler how far it was to Mona (Anglesey). Being a cobbler, the stranger was carrying a whole load of worn out shoes in a trolley and, as he was also a bit of a joker, told the couple that he had worn out all the shoes walking *from* Mona. This reply did not go down at all well with our giants, being very weary and footsore from having carried their load of stones so far. On hearing the cobbler's story, they threw down their stones where they stood, thus creating Barclodiad y Gawres and therefore the 'Giantess's Apronful'.

14. Llys Llewelyn Heritage Centre

Llys Llewelyn Heritage Centre

In many years of travelling around Anglesey, I had found this south-eastern corner of the island to be a desert for refreshment stops, until in 2005 I finally found the public conveniences at Llys Llewelyn, in the town of Aberffraw, to be open and this has became a regular break on tours since. Then on a recent research trip, to my surprise, I found that the full Llys Llewelyn Heritage Centre had opened.

It was a satisfying experience to view the facilities for the first time and an experience that I wholeheartedly recommend. There is a small museum and display room, with historical and archaeological exhibits from around the island, together with paintings from local artists. In a side room, an extremely well put together audio-visual film takes you through a useful potted history of the island. Then of course there is the gift shop, with books, maps, trinkets and drinks etc. You will find a café in a separate building, which effectively completes the visit to this fine resource.

15. St Cwyfan's Church in the Sea
OS-114-337684

St Cwyfan's Church in the Sea

Leaving the Llys Llewelyn Heritage Centre and the village of Aberffraw, you follow a long narrow winding road with high hedgerows and very few passing places, down to Porth Cwyfan, where the road comes to an abrupt end, leaving you facing the open sea. The end of the road here has cut into the soft sandy earth over the years and this has created two high banks and a natural slipway between, used by a constant troop of surfers.

The Church of St Cwyfan sits on a mini-island surrounded by a thick brick wall to protect against further erosion, which is already responsible for creating the island and isolating the church. St Cwyfan's used to stand on a mainland cliff overlooking both Porth Cwyfan and Porth China, and maps from the early 17th century still show the headland as connected. Unfortunately, the boulder clay foundation was no defence from the constant tides and the island, now called 'Cribinau', was created. At low tide it is still possible to reach the church down a narrow causeway, and services are held regularly on the first Sunday in June and August; if you would like a romantic place to get married, you can book the church for a special service and some of the local children are still christened here.

A new church was opened on the mainland in 1871 and St Cwyfan's, being abandoned to the elements, quickly went into disrepair, losing its roof and becoming generally saturated. The church has had three champions in its long history, the first of which was St Cwyfan himself in the 7th Century and then two much more recently. Harold Hughes, a well known architect from Llanfairfechan, ploughed money into restoring of the roof and the main body of the church and built the protecting wall around the island. Then in 2005, Cadw produced a grant of £16,500 to renovate St Cwyfan's for posterity, and the planned works involved repairs to the external walls, the installation of new leaded glazing, some internal decoration and also whitewashing the external brickwork with protecting lime to match many other churches in Wales.

View of St Cwyfan's Bay and Church from the end of the road

This last item was the cause of much turmoil in the local community, who had become used to the church in its bare and rugged form. According to BBC Wales News on Wednesday, November 2nd 2005, Dr Greg Stevenson from the department of archaeology and anthropology at the University of Wales, Lampeter, said "the location of the church meant it was at the mercy of the sea and weather". He added that "the site's authenticity also had to be taken into account. There would have been lime render both inside and out originally, it would not have been stripped until Victorian times. Historically it is completely wrong as it is now". This seemed to clinch the deal, the deed was done and today the results are quite striking. It is interesting that these early Christian buildings were given this bright white appearance, much in the same way that ancient monuments such as henges and chambered tombs would have been coated with a layer of gypsum, to provide a magnificent glow for miles around.

St Cwyfan (498-618 AD) is said to have lived for 120 years, which earned him the position of patron saint of longevity. He is thought to have been born an Irishman with the name of St Kevin of Glendalough in County Wicklow. After moving to North Wales and settling in a hermitage near a spectacular waterfall in the town of Dyserth, in Denbighshire. We have been visiting Dyserth on tours for many years and I can recommend that you call off there if you are ever passing through North Wales, perhaps on the main A55 coast road. Just down the road from Dyserth is Maen Achwyfan, one of the most important ancient crosses in Britain which is connected to St Cwyfan through its old name of Maen Cwyfan, or Cwyfan's stone.

St Cwyfan became a follower of the Welsh monk, St Beuno Gasulsych, and travelled the Celtic areas of Northern Britain, eventually founding his church on Anglesey in the early 7th century. Originally it would have been a wattle and daub construction and the present structure dates back to the 12th

century, when the economy on the island resulted in the construction of many stone churches, like the ones at Din Lligwy and the church of St Seiriol, for example. Then in the 14th century the body of the church was again modified resulting in the main structure we see today.

16. Llangadwaladr Church of St Cadwaladr and the Stone of St Cadfan

OS-114-384693

Llangaðwalaðr Church of St Caðwalaðr

The Llangadwaladr church of St Cadwaladr is in the hamlet of Llangadwaladr, a little further east along the A4080 from Aberffraw. The original name of the church was 'Eglwys Ael', meaning 'Wattle Church', which reflects its original purpose as a Royal monastery, being built around 615 AD. There is a small car park provided just for the church with a large gate, so visitors have the job of opening and closing it on arrival and leaving. Then, as you walk through a second gate, you are provided with an idyllic view of old Britain, with the church sitting at the end a long path through the graveyard. Everything inside is in proportion, with the long nave and the ornate transept filling the requirements of the eye-pleasing 'golden section' that can be found throughout nature.

Soon after the Romans left Britain, the ensuing power vacuum was filled by the return of the British kings. Aberffraw was the capital of the kingdom of Gwynedd and the home of King Cadwallon, who died in 634 AD leaving a one year old son and heir. This son was Cadwaladr Fendigaid, who was to become St Cadwaladr the Blessed and who had to be taken in to exile in Brittany to avoid a civil war in Gwynedd, which put King Cadfael Cadomedd - the Battle-Shirker - (633-664) on the throne.

During Cadfael's reign, Gwynedd suffered from famine, followed by the plague and it is probable that it was this that caused the king's death in 664 AD. With the throne vacant again, Cadwaladr sent his son Idwal Iwrch - the Roebuck - (650-712), back from Brittany to claim it before following him home to Aberffraw. On returning to Gwynedd, Cadwaladr became a patron of the church, especially focusing on Clynnog Fawr Abbey on the north coast of the Llyn Peninsula in north-west Wales, founded by Beuno the mentor of St Cwyfan. Some Welsh manuscripts state that the Abbot of Clynnog was given a seat at the court of the king of Gwynedd. It is possible that Cadwaladr became a monk at the Eglwys Ael monastery towards the end of his life and he died during a pilgrimage to Rome on November 12th 682 AD. He was buried at Eglwys Ael, which then took the name 'Llangadwaladr' – meaning 'church of Cadwaladr' – in his memory.

The Stone of St Cadfan

The Church of St Cadwaladr is also famous for being the resting place of King Cadfan of Gwynedd, the Grandfather of Cadwaladr the Blessed, who died in 625 AD. His memorial stone was found somewhere in the vicinity of the church and can now be seen set into the wall opposite the door. The strange inscription reads "King Cadfan, the Wisest and Most Renowned of All Kings Lies Here", with a cross added to the right of the plaque, in the centre. This a real piece of history going back nearly 1,400 years and gazing upon it almost brings you within the walls of the ancient court of the kings of Gwynedd.

The Stone of St Cadfan

17. Din Dryfol Burial Chamber
OS-114-395725

Din Dryfol Burial Chamber

Din Dryfol (pronounced 'Din Drivvle') is one of the more unusual sites on Anglesey and it is definitely amongst the hardest to find. Luckily, it is plotted on the Ordnance Survey map (Landranger 114) as 'Burial Chamber', right next to the name 'Din Dryfol', which helps you find the general area, but is not a great deal of help when it comes to locating the actual site.

Continuing easterly on the A4080 from the village of Llangadwaladr, the road takes a sharp turn to the left, before taking you to a T junction. Take the right hand fork here onto the B4422 through the tiny hamlet of Bethel and the third turning on the left takes you onto another of Anglesey's narrow roads, with the typical high hedgerows and in this case, not many passing places. If fate does deliver you an obstruction in the form of a tractor approaching from the opposite direction, your only available sanctuary here is to be found by tucking closely into the odd field entrance. This is not always easy when you are in the process of negotiating the labyrinthine country roads in a large minibus with a dozen back-seat drivers, who are more than willing to offer advice at any point of difficulty.

Fortunately, the narrow lane ends after a few hundred yards and it widens out to form the courtyard of a large modern house. Initially, this road's abrupt termination on private land, with no indication as to the direction of the burial chamber is disconcerting. On my reconnaissance visit to Din Dryfol, the extremely helpful and friendly lady of the house soon rectified this situation by pointing me in the direction of a chained gate to the right of the yard and provided me with precise directions to the site. Having climbed over the gate, the path leads over rough undergrowth comprised of wild grasses and fern, towards a massive steep sided rocky outcrop, which luckily you don't have to climb. Following the path until it splits at the foot of the tumulus, the right fork leads round to the far side where the tomb sits on a raised shelf overlooking the plains to the northwest.

Din Dryfol's isolated location adds to the lamentable atmosphere of the area surrounding the site. Anyone coming across Din Dryfol whilst out for a ramble or dog walking trek, with no knowledge of the site or of pre-history, would probable continue right past without noticing this 5,000 year old monument, as its appearance and structure are far from obvious.

The site is perched on a flat rocky strip and is ideally located to take advantage of the natural features of the landscape. Having seen many ancient sites throughout Europe, my mind tends to piece the situation together and build a picture when looking at a sacred area. Din Dryfol is no exception and it is easy to imagine this as an early holy place used for meetings by hunter-gatherer communities before they turned to farming and largely lost their nomadic spirit. The hill standing high behind the chamber to the southeast would have been recognisable on the horizon for many miles around and a fire on its summit would have acted as a beacon drawing people towards it for mooting. At the edge of the strip plateau a rocky band would have proved useful for gathering crowds to take position ready for the proceedings to take place on this early Gorsedd or 'throne'. It cannot help but produce a feeling of nostalgia to think that this would still be happening – in much the same way as the subjects of the kings of Gwynedd gathered in nearby Aberffraw – so many thousands of years later.

It would not have been until around 3,000 BC that monuments of this sort began adorning the landscapes of Britain and Din Dryfol would have been a prime example in its heyday. The long linear form of the main structure is still apparent today, although all but two of the upright megaliths have disappeared over the millennia. The first stone you see, as you approach the site on the fern- walled path around the hillock, is a narrow-bladed portal stone in the shape of a capped pyramid. There are none of the original curbstones left that would have once covered the tomb chambers, but an excavation in 1969 and 1970 indicated that the site would have been constructed over various time periods, resulting in four rectangular chambers. Along with a collection of pottery shards, the most unusual item recovered by the dig is a wooden portal, a unique feature in sites of this sort.

In its completed form the tomb would have appeared as a 200 foot long cairn stretching the length of the narrow rocky platform. The well-preserved chambered tomb on the Isle of Man, Cashtal yn Ard, would probably have looked similar to Din Dryfol, and it provides a visual aid to the imagination. At Cashtal yn Ard, you can still see the ritual area, outlined by a curved semi-circular line of standing megaliths. Behind this is a neat row of clearly defined chambers indicated by stone slabs, which, although they have also lost their capstones, are none the less still in extremely good condition.

18. Oriel Ynys Mon

Oriel Ynys Mon - Museum of Anglesey

Of all the museums and visitor centres on Anglesey, Oriel Ynys Mon (meaning Museum of Anglesey), is the star of the show and an absolute must for anyone visiting the island's sites. The museum opened in 1991 and I have been visiting the amenities here on the outskirts of Llangefni for many years and have watched it expand to what is today a large multifaceted facility for all categories of visitors from locals to international tourists.

Llangefni is easily reached and is an ideal location for the museum, being only seven and a half miles from the bridges onto the island. It is also connected to the main A55 and A5, which runs south of the town less than two miles away, by both the A5114 and the B4422. Arriving in Llangefni, it is a simple matter to follow the brown signs to 'Oriel Ynys Mon', on the northern edge of the town. The car park is huge and accessible and provides entrance to the whole building, including the museum and art galleries, which are free of charge. To the left of the main doorway, a good starting point is the relaxing Blas Mwy Café, where you can buy a whole selection of snacks, main meals and drinks, including some tasty homemade local specials. Opposite the café is the Jac Do shop selling the usual gifts along with local books, crafts and cards. Since the introduction of a programme of expansion of the whole of Oriel Ynys Mon in 2008, a small exhibition space has been created, called the Y Nyth, selling a collection of original works of art by local artists.

The main exhibit rooms include four art gallery spaces, displaying both a changing programme of exhibits and a collection of work by Sir Kyffin Williams, a patron of the Welsh arts, who was a supporter of the Oriel Ynys Mon until his death in 2006, and who had a hand in its design. The Oriel Kyffin Williams Gallery is the permanent home to more than 400 donated works by the artist and is a tribute to his contribution to Welsh art.

The History Gallery is a must for anyone interested in Anglesey's cultural and historical development. The hall covers the prehistory of the island and the reconstruction of Barclodiad y Gawres chambered tomb. Evidence discovered during excavations provides a great insight into life at ancient sites. Other exhibits and artefacts cover various time periods, including the beginnings and growth of tourism and a permanent display of the work of the wildlife artist Charles F. Tunnicliffe, which records Anglesey's flora, fauna and living history.

19. Caer Leb Ancient Settlement
OS-114-473675

Caer Leb Ancient Settlement

On visiting the remains of the ancient settlement at Caer Leb, the tour of Anglesey, as followed over the previous chapters, has nearly come full circle. The site is easily accessible a few hundred yards down a narrow road off the south-eastern section of the A4080, quite near to Castell Bryn Gwyn. It is signposted from the main road and the small lay-by style car park is easily found. The short walk from the road follows a stream through a field, and it quickly becomes obvious that this is semi-marshland. If the landscape here is unchanged since the settlement was inhabited, this would have been a damp place to live, but with plenty of essential fresh water.

In its present state, Caer Leb appears as a set of earthworked lines creating a rectangular enclosure some 200 feet in length and 160 feet in width, with a portal entrance in the centre of one of the shorter banks. The settlement used to be surrounded by two full defensive banks, with a deep ditch between, but the north and east sides of the outer bank have long since disappeared. The ditch gets quite wet and boggy, especially in the winter months, and this had led to suggestions that it was in fact a moat, although this does not seem particularly likely and no real evidence of this unusual feature has ever been found.

The on-site Cadw information board shows an interesting illustration of a reconstructed settlement, produced from evidence uncovered at an 1865 excavation. The remains of at least two roundhouses with laid stone flag floors and fireplaces were found, together with a rectangular building near the entrance. The various artefacts discovered during the excavations at Caer Leb, and at a similar site called Din yn Eryr, just inland from Beaumaris, have assisted in putting a date of early occupation of the site as long ago as the second century BC, and therefore Iron Age. A room found at the Din Lligwy settlement with a comparable shape to the rectangular one at Caer Leb has been recorded as being used as a foundry, and the Iron Age date attributed to this site may indicate such a use here, although no evidence of this has been found. This room could also have been used a storage area, such as the ones at the Holyhead Mountain settlement site or maybe simply as an animal enclosure.

The excavation at Caer Leb recorded a brooch from the 3rd Century AD, a 4th Century Denarius of Postumus, Roman pottery and grind tools, known as quern-stones. A medieval coin has also been found on a platform along the north-east side of the enclosure. All this would indicate that Caer Leb had been continually occupied until the 4th century AD, some 700 years.

20. Plas Newydd

OS-114-521696

Plas Newydd is a magnificent gothic mansion sitting on the banks of the Menai Strait with a history going back to the 15th century. At that time, the estate was in the hands of the Griffiths family from Bangor, who owned much of Anglesey. The estate today is the home of the Marquess of Anglesey and is in the care of the National Trust, who can arrange visits to the two chambered tombs in the gardens. The estate can be reached from the A4080 half a mile after the turning to Bryn Celli Ddu, on the way into the town which goes by the name of Llanfairpwllgwyngyllgogerychwyrndrobwllllantysiliogogogoch at the end of the Britannia Bridge.

Plas Newydd can boast some influential and celebrated residents over its 600 year history. In the late 1600s, it was home to Nicholas Bayly, Gentleman of the Chamber to King Charles II, who made him Governor of Galway and the isles of Aran in Galway Bay. Nicholas's son Edward was made the first baronet of Plas Newydd in 1730, and this monumental rise in fortunes was furthered in turn Edward's son, also called Nicholas, who married into the Paget family of Staffordshire in the second half of the 18th century. This was a powerful connection as William, 1st Baron Paget, had been a chief advisor to King Henry VIII.

Another of Plas Newydd's illustrious inhabitants was Henry William Paget, the Duke of Wellington's second in command, who distinguished himself at the battle of Waterloo and, as a result, was made the 1st Marquess of Anglesey. A memorial column to Henry William was erected in Llanfair Pwllgwyngyll in 1817, which, unlike the one in Trafalgar Square, can be climbed via its 115 steps to take advantage of the panoramic views of North Wales. The present statue was added in 1860, six years after the death of the Marquess at the age of 85.

The house today is open to the public and holds a collection of work by the artist Rex Whistler, who had been an associate and friend of the 6th Marquess. One of Whistler's finest works on show in the house is a 58 foot long mural painted for the Marquess, which depicts a Mediterranean harbour scene. The painting was fixed to the dining room wall at Plas Newydd next to a large window overlooking the Menai Strait so that the observer can compare a Welsh sea view with one of the hot south.

Also on display in the house is a military exhibition with records of the military exploits of the family, together with a collection of medals, military uniforms and paintings of war scenes.

Bryn yr Hen Bobl Burial Chamber
OS-114-519689

Bryn yr Hen Bobl entrance portal

Because of its unique structure, Bryn yr Hen Bobl is a significant, if slightly estranged, member of Anglesey's burial chamber family. It is one of the least accessible on the island, hiding on private land in the grounds of Plas Newydd. Like its sister site, Bryn Celli Ddu less than a mile to the north, Bryn yr Bobl still retains its mound of curbstones covered in earth and was until recently, adorned with two tall ash trees sitting on its summit, spreading their spider's web of roots around the slopes. Unfortunately these two trees had to be felled as one had died, but others are already appearing to take their place. The sprouting of trees out of heaps or embankments of stones is a repeating feature amongst the ancient sites of Britain; it appears as if the spaces between the stones provide an ideal spot for the young saplings to take root.

The cairn at Bryn yr Bobl is an unusual kidney shape, measuring some 130 feet by 100 feet and with a height of over 15 feet. It is internally supported by two stone walls around the edges and it contains a rectangular stone chamber of around six feet by three feet, facing to the east with views across the Menai Strait and over to the mainland and the Snowdon range. The capstone, which measures around nine feet by six feet, has split into two halves at some unrecorded time long ago and is open to the elements. As with many sites of its type, a wide forecourt and ritual area stands in front of the entrance, where the remnants of four fires have been found next to a small megalith, which was probably used as a blocking stone to close off the opening to the chamber.

Early reports of the existence of Bryn yr Hen Bobl were made as early as 1549 by John Leyland, antiquary to Henry VIII, while the first published account did not appear until Henry Rowlands' *Mona Antiqua Restaurata* (1723); an excavation did not take place until 1929-35, when W. J. Hemp dug there. In his findings, published in 1936, Hemp recorded finding a broken oval section of bone pin, together with a selection of bone fragments from around twenty adults and children of both sexes in the chamber itself. The English translation of Bryn yr Hen Bobl, is 'Hill of the Old People' suggesting a holy place where the ancestors would have been remembered in rituals at certain important times of the yearly cycle. Further evidence of this is indicated by the presence of pottery shards found in the remains of the forecourt fires, suggesting the presence of ceremony.

More pottery and flint was found in the chamber and around the general area than in any other excavation on the island, which would suggest an area of continual usage that was probably the location of an ancient settlement.

A visitor to Bryn yr Hen Bobl at the time of writing would find a neglected site in need of cleaning up and general maintenance. The sheep in the field keep the surrounding grass short, but the portal entrance is overgrown. A fence was erected in 2009, to protect the forecourt and chamber area and to prevent anyone from falling off the capstone, so maybe this wonderful ancient place of meeting, ceremony and respect for the ancestors is about to get the attention it deserves.

Plas Newydd Burial Chamber
OS-114-520697

Plas Newydd takes its name from the stately home in whose grounds this rather haphazard yet magnificent chambered tomb sits, surrounded by immaculately manicured lawns. It is difficult to say if the two chambers are in their original situation or whether some repositioning and reconstruction work was carried out when the estate gardens were landscaped in the 18th century. Possible evidence of this may be seen in the position of the megaliths supporting the heaviest part of the capstone on the largest chamber to the north. This gigantic slab rests on four stones on its outer edge, one of which appears to have been placed diagonally as a prop, a method of positioning that is highly unusual on monuments in their original state.

The second chamber to the south is the much smaller of the two and the tiny compartment, which supports its own capstone, is covered in ivy and unfortunately graffiti in the shape of a box design which has been sprayed in red paint to the rear of the space. This is particularly disappointing when considering that the chambered tombs at Plas Newydd are amongst the most difficult to reach, being on private land, and that the many sites which are readily available to the public are generally graffiti-free and respected by their many visitors.

Plas Newydd Burial Chamber

Plas Newydd's positioning on a north-east to south-west axis, and the direction of slope of the largest capstone over the main chamber, would suggest an alignment to the midsummer sunrise, in the same way as its nearby partner Bryn Celli Ddu. In its present state, the lack of a portal entrance to the north-east would appear incorrect and this could again be further evidence of tampering with the position of the supporting megaliths.

Map of Anglesey

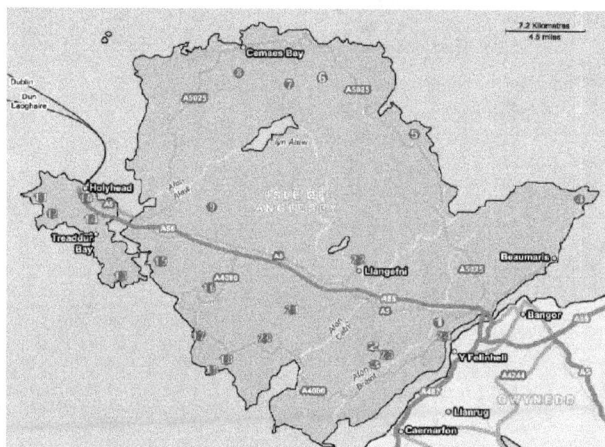

1 Bryn Celli Ddu Chambered Tomb

2 Bodowyr Cromlech

3 Bryn Gwyn Area

4 Holy Penmon

5 Lligwy Region

6 Parys Mountain Copper Mine

7 Bodewryd Stone

8 Mein Hirion Standing Stones

9 Presaddfed Chambered Tomb

10 St Cybi's Church

11 Holyhead Mountain Settlement

12 Penrhos Feilw Standing Stones

13 Rhoscolyn Burial Chamber

14 Trefignath Chambered Cairn &
   Mawr Standing Stone

15 Llyn Cerrig Bach

16 Ty Newydd Burial Chamber

17 Barclodiad y Gawres

18 Llys Llewelyn Heritage Centre

19 St Cwyfan's Church in the Sea

20 Church of St Cadwaladr & the Stone
   of St Cadfan

21 Din Dryfol Burial Chamber

22 Oriel Ynys Mon

23 Caer Leb Ancient Settlement

24 Plas Newydd Estate

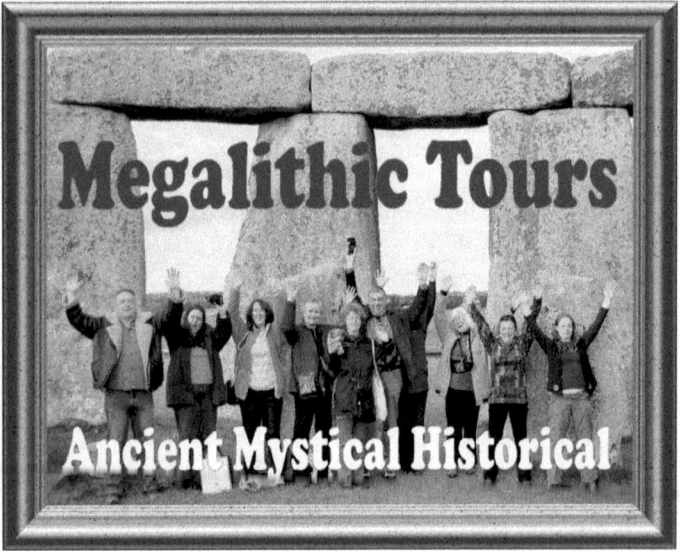

Megalithic Tours

Neil McDonald BA (Hons)

01772 728181
07799 061991

neil@megalithictours.com

50 Cottam Avenue
Ingol
Preston
Lancashire
PR2 3XH

www.megalithictours.com

www.ingramcontent.com/pod-product-compliance
Lightning Source LLC
Chambersburg PA
CBHW060949040426
42445CB00011B/1077